Pronouns

© 2015 OnBoard Academics, Inc
Portsmouth, NH
800-596-3175
www.onboardacademics.com
ISBN: 978-1-63096-033-9

ALL RIGHTS RESERVED. This book contains material protected under International and Federal Copyright Laws and Treaties. Any unauthorized reprint or use of this material is prohibited. No part of this book may be reproduced or transmitted in any form or by any means, electronic or mechanical, including photocopying, reprinting, recording, or by any information storage and retrieval system without expressed written permission from the author / publisher.

OnBoard Academic's books are specifically designed to be used as printed workbooks or as on-screen instruction. Each page offers focused exercises and students quickly master topics with enough proficiency to move on to the next level.

OnBoard Academic's lessons are used in over 25,000 classrooms to rave reviews. Our lessons are aligned to the most recent governmental standards and are updated from time to time as standards change. Correlation documents are located on our website. Our lessons are created, edited and evaluated by educators to ensure top quality and real life success.

Interactive lessons for digital whiteboards, mobile devices, and PCs are available at www.onboardacademics.com. These interactive lessons make great additions to our books.

You can always reach us at customerservice@onboardacademics.com.

OnBoard Academics Workbook   K-2 ELA

Pronoun

Key Vocabulary

noun

pronoun

singular

plural

I'm making a home movie!
Fill in the blanks with pronouns.

 This is Tori. _____ plays a diamond thief.

 This is Fernando. _____ plays a detective.

 This is Owen, Mia and me. _____ play security guards at the museum.

 These are some of my other friends. _____ are extras in the movie.

  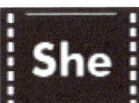 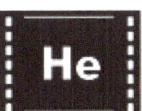

A pronoun takes the place of a noun.

Why do you think we use pronouns?

Pronoun or noun?
Sort the words.

pronouns	nouns

man	girl	it	they
she	he	puppy	friend
nurse	us	we	kitten

Who is he?

Alison and Owen were on a walk.
"Look at that bird over there," Alison said.
"Wow, that's so cool," he shouted.

Who is "he"?

Owen   **Alison**   **The bird**

_____

Sort the words.
Pronouns can be singular or they can be plural.

🙂 singular	🙂🙂 plural

we	them	him	they
she	it	he	us

Fill in the missing pronouns.

My brother, Owen, plays on a baseball team called the Blues. _____ plays first base. My friend, Tori, is also on the team. _____ is a pitcher. _____ play every Saturday. My Dad and _____ have been to every game this season. _____ are the Blues' biggest fans!

OnBoard Academics Workbook   K-2 ELA

Name_____

Pronouns Quiz

1. A pronoun is an action word. True or false?

2. Fill in the blank. _____ both have the same first name.
    a. He
    b. She
    c. It
    d. We

3. Fill in the blank. _____ are identical twins.
    a. Them
    b. They
    c. She
    d. It

4. Circle the singular pronouns.
    a. he
    b. they
    c. them
    d. we

OnBoard Academics Workbook Grade 4 ELA

Contractions and Possessive Pronouns

Key Vocabulary

contraction

possessive noun

possessive pronoun

Contractions

Mia said that she **does not** understand contractions.

A **contraction** is a single word made by combining two other words using an apostrophe in place of letters from the original words. A contraction takes its name from the verb *to contract*, meaning to shrink or reduce in size.

Mia said that she **doesn't** understand contractions.

OnBoard Academics Workbook — Grade 4 ELA

Complete these contractions.

do	+	not	=	
should	+	not	=	
have	+	not	=	
could	+	not	=	
can	+	not	=	
will	+	not	=	

Am, is and are contractions

Am, is and *are* contractions are formed by replacing the first vowel in the verb with an apostrophe.

Complete these am, is and are contractions.

do	+	not	=	
should	+	not	=	
have	+	not	=	
could	+	not	=	
can	+	not	=	
will	+	not	=	

OnBoard Academics Workbook — Grade 4 ELA

Have, has and had contractions

> *Have, has,* and *had* contractions are formed by replacing the -ha with an apostrophe.

Complete these, have, has and had contractions.

I	+	have	=
you	+	had	=
she	+	has	=
we	+	had	=
they	+	have	=
it	+	has	=

©2013 OnBoard Academics, Inc. www.onboardacademics.com

OnBoard Academics Workbook

Grade 4 ELA

It's and Its

Remember to check you use of it and it's by saying the sentence and replacing "it is" whenever it's or its is used. If "it is" makes sense, then the answer is it's.

The bone is in [its] mouth.

Yes, and [it's] a big one.

_____

Contraction or possessive pronoun?
Fill in the blanks.

My phone keeps losing [   ] charge.

Well, that's because [   ] an old model.

You should change [   ] phone.

You can change it for free if [   ] on a contract.

Come on, [   ] able to afford a contract?

Just kids [   ] parents pay for [   ] phone.

And [   ] the ones that have unlimited texts, too!

| it's | your | their | who's |
| its | you're | they're | whose |

©2013 OnBoard Academics, Inc.   www.onboardacademics.com

OnBoard Academics Workbook — Grade 4 ELA

Fill in the blank.

I didn't realize _____ his cousin.

Do you know _____ is coaching the team?

The laptop has lost _____ internet connection.

My parents are celebrating _____ anniversary.

But it's ours not _____.

your	you're
who's	whose
its	it's
they're	their
there's	theirs

Name_____

Contractions and Possessive Pronouns Quiz

1. The word it's is always a contraction. True or false?

2. Which sentence is not correct?
    a. They're parents are both doctors.
    b. When the dog growled, I saw its sharp teeth.
    c. I's not ours; i's theirs.
    d. You mustn't ride your bike at night without lights.

3. Which sentence is correct?
    a. Whose next in line?
    b. Your genes are unique.
    c. We waited by they're house.
    d. It's okay to say your sorry sometimes.

4. _____ coming to the game too!
    a. They're
    b. Their
    c. There
    d. Theirs

5. _____ jacket is this?
    a. Whose
    b. Who's

©2013 OnBoard Academics, Inc.   www.onboardacademics.com

OnBoard Academics Workbook   Grade 3 ELA

Using I and me

Key Vocabulary

Pronoun

Subject Predicate

OnBoard Academics Workbook — Grade 3 ELA

Using the pronouns I and me.
Study the passage below and notice the difference between I and me.

> The **subject** is who or what a sentence is about. The **predicate** tells us what the subject is or does. Notice the *I* and the *me* in each sentence.

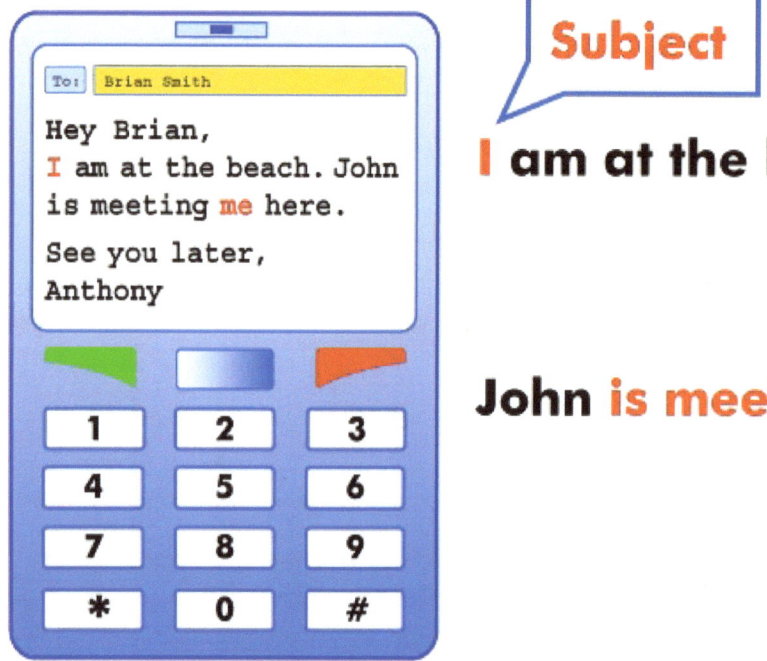

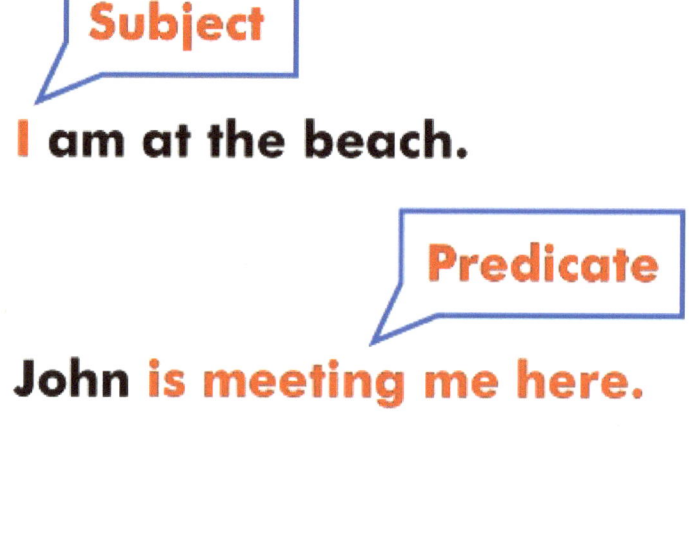

Subject

I am at the beach.

Predicate

John is meeting me here.

©2013 OnBoard Academics, Inc.   www.onboardacademics.com

OnBoard Academics Workbook — Grade 3 ELA

Separate the subject and the predicate and identify the pronoun.

Follow the example.

My mom drove me here.

My brother and I played in the sand.

Subject	Predicate	I	me
I	am at the beach.		

Use the pronoun **I** in the *subject* of a sentence.
Use the pronoun **me** in the *predicate* of a sentence.

©2013 OnBoard Academics, Inc.   www.onboardacademics.com

OnBoard Academics Workbook

Grade 3 ELA

Determine whether the pronoun (I or me) is the subject or predicate part of the sentence.

Label the box next to the sentence.

My dad and I went to the game this weekend.

Hey, why didn't you call me?

I thought you were visiting your grandmother.

She called me to say she wasn't feeling well.

subject   **predicate**

OnBoard Academics Workbook

Grade 3 ELA

Add the pronoun in the box within the sentence and identify whether it is in the subject or predicate part of the sentence by indicating P or S in the box after the sentence.

☐ like solving puzzles. ☐

People always give them to ☐ . ☐

Carla gave ☐ a whole book of puzzles. ☐

My mom and ☐ will do them together. ☐

©2013 OnBoard Academics, Inc.   www.onboardacademics.com

OnBoard Academics Workbook — Grade 3 ELA

Using I or me.
Enter your answer in the gold box.

> Say the sentence without "and" and the other person's name to help determine if you need **I** or **me**.

1 Jenna sits behind James and .

Jenna sits behind James and **I?**
or
Jenna sits behind James and **me?**

2 Owen and  studied for hours.

Owen and **I studied for hours?**
or
Owen and **me studied for hours?**

OnBoard Academics Workbook

Grade 3 ELA

Identify the sentences that use the pronouns I and me correctly by placing a check in the box next to the sentence. If used incorrectly, mark the box with an X.

	Dad gave the keys to Larry and I.	☐
	Aunt Lucy and I went dress shopping.	☐
	Sam and me ran to the bus.	☐
	Mr. Smith and I went over my homework.	☐
	Dad ordered a pizza for Jane and me.	☐

©2013 OnBoard Academics, Inc.   www.onboardacademics.com

Fill in the blanks with the appropriate pronouns.
You may use the suggestions under the passage.

Mom gave _____ the grocery list, and she asked ____ to clip the coupons. After _____ had finished the shopping, ____ realized we had forotten to bring the coupons.

| Mia and I | I |
| Mia and me | me |

Name_____

Using I and me Quiz

1. True or false? We use the pronoun me in the subject of a sentence.

2. Circle the sentence that is written correctly.
    a. I and Henry went to the mall.
    b. Henry and me went too the mall.
    c. Henry and I went to the mall.
    d. Me and Henry went to the mall.

3. Circle the sentence that is written correctly.
    a. Aunt Martha's pie tasted good to I.
    b. Me enjoyed Aunt Martha's pie.
    c. I enjoyed Aunt Martha's pie.
    d. Aunt Martha gave I a delicious pie.

4. Circle the sentence not written correctly.
    a. Rob and me are eating dinner.
    b. Rob and I are eating dinner.
    c. Rob is eating dinner with me.
    d. I am eating dinner with Rob.

5. Fill in the blank with I or me. Patty was speaking to my friend and _____.